A Bridge to the Other Side:

Channeled messages of death and life.

୨ଚ

Medium Laura Evans

Edited by Priya Verma

Copyright 2010 Medium Laura Evans.
All rights reserved. No part of this publication may be reproduced, stored in a retrieval system, or transmitted in any form or by any means, electronic, mechanical, recording or otherwise, without the prior written permission of the author.

ISBN   1453621520

EAN-13   9781453621523

Table of Contents

DEDICATION — 6

FOREWORD — 8

MESSAGE TO THE READER — 10

ABOUT THE AUTHOR — 12

A MESSAGE FOR THOSE WHO ARE GRIEVING — 22

IS DEATH THE END? — 24

REINCARNATION? TO BE BORN AGAIN. WHY? — 26

GUIDES THAT ARE OUR PREVIOUS FAMILY — 28

FAITH WITHOUT SEEING — 29

WHEN OPPORTUNITY KNOCKS, — 31

YOUR PATH?	33
ANGELIC HANDS	35
HEALING THE WORLD WITH JOY	37
CALL TO US	38
QUESTIONS AND ANSWERS WITH SPIRIT	43

Dedication

To my mother and father – Shirley and Carl Altz - Thank you for giving me the wings to fly and the support to be anything I wanted to be. You are truly missed Papa and I love you mom.

My brothers James and Jack and sister Colleen - thank you for believing in me, even when you didn't want to.

To my grandparents on the Other Side, Jean Altz, Carl Altz Sr., Thelma Pringle and Herbert Desotell– You all have helped me believe!

To my children, Savana Rain and Dakota Storm - you have inspired me more than you know - Thank you for picking me to be your mother.

Scott Evans - you always knew that I could be so much more than I ever did and I thank you for that.

To Nat Gewanter - you never fail to see the positive in everything, even me! Thank you for being my best friend, my sounding board, my playmate and my love. I love you mostest ostest!

To Lauren Lewis , Lori Brewer and the "Glitz" girls - without you I would have never "come out of my broom closet". You all are my greatest fans and beloved friends.

To Priya Verma, UK, my closest friend and my student; keep listening with your heart and reaching for the stars!!

To my former co-workers at POH VA Clinic – I miss you guys!

To my fellow mediums and friends: Jodi Livon, Karen Anderson, Michael Carbone, Karen Dawson, Mandy Jooste, and way too many more to mention as well as all the wonderful people I got to meet through hosting a radio show on BlogTalk!

May God and the angels continue to bless all of you in your lives.

Foreword

"Spirit guide" is a term used by the Western tradition of Spiritualist Churches, mediums, and psychics to describe an entity that remains a disincarnate spirit in order to act as a spiritual counselor or protector to a living incarnated human being.

According to theosophical doctrine, spirit guides are persons who have lived many former lifetimes, paid their karmic debts, and advanced beyond a need to reincarnate. Each is assigned to watch over an incarnate person, not only on this Earth, but on other planets throughout the universe. Many psychics believe that spirit guides are chosen on "the other side" by us and God before we incarnate and that they guide us to follow our life's plan because we want them to.

Some people claim it is possible to meet one's spirit guide in dreams or on the astral plane.

You were drawn to this book because you are ready to undertake a journey to find your true purpose on this earth. To understand the reasons we go through trauma, illness, pain, loss, poverty and more. This book is to help you look past your ego of self doubt and negative thoughts to discover the light being that exists inside.

I hope you enjoy it as much as I have. Each page came to life by the thoughts and feelings of spirit guides, angels and light beings. I do not take credit for their work, I simply am the instrument and they are the music.

Most of the time, my channeled messages are from a collected group of souls. They have used my hands but these are their teachings.

(The text that has been italicized are the words that have been channeled through me by spirit. Normal text writings are the thoughts and views of me, the author.)

Message to the Reader

From the Angels

Although there are other books which have been written by spirit beings, this book is more for the beginner. We have targeted you who are just awakening to the fact that there are unseen forces here to help you when you need it.

Knowing that you are never alone in your life is something we wish to teach everyone. We would like everyone to be able to accept the divine light and spread joy and love to those who are dark in mind. Each holds this divine light inside them. It is up to you to quiet the ego which precipitates fear, greed and its own protection and use the divine light of knowing; to know that you are worthy of our help and support. To know that when you feel no one loves you, you are wrong. We all love you no matter what. Nothing you can do or say will ever change that.

The world is going through a shift of awareness. The depression and malice that exists is because of negative thoughts breeding throughout your world. We light beings are building our legions of light workers within all of you. Positive thoughts of love and joy are the only weapons against the destruction of the souls that are incarnate on earth.

In the pages of this book you will find many examples of our encouragement to keep you positive and happy in order to fulfill the shift throughout mankind. Some words may make you feel that you have known these answers all along and some, because of your ego's fear, will be new to you and maybe even frightening. Do not let the fear take hold. Fear is destructive to your divine light and will work very hard to give you reasons to not believe in the light.

Know that you were all born of God and your Creator wants universal light and love for all of you. You are chosen. You are the key to stop war, violence against mankind, destruction, greed and abuse. Your effort whether you believe is small or not, has an enormous impact on creating this happiness; where when a stone is dropped into a lake, the ripples cascade out, in a multitude of rings. So does your kindness to a child, an elderly person, a homeless person, an angry person and so on. You give your love and light to them and this ripples into them. They may then hug someone they have argued with in the past, call an old friend and bring joy to that person's life as well. Ripple out positive loving vibrations and your efforts will be matched and duplicated.

You may be a beginner in the beliefs of light workers, spirit guides and heavenly aid, but to us, you have just forgotten what you already knew. You learned much from your past lives and from your home here. Above all things, Love is the answer.

~ *Angels of the Divine Purpose*

About the Author

I was born psychic/medium. Talking to my "imaginary friends" was something I was accustomed to and no one ever told me it was wrong. Sure I was a normal kid too. I played cops and robbers, dress-up and such, but I also played "cards" with my mom too. We would have a stack of cards with colored circles on one side and a crazy black and white pattern on the back. I never knew my mother was "training" my psychic senses. I just knew it was a lot of fun to get 48/50 cards right!

When my father's mother, Jean, passed away I was 5 years old. She was in a coma after having a massive heart attack. She had come to me while we were vacationing in Hawaii; I remember waking up and looking for her that morning – thinking she had flown in to see us. She came to tell me that she had to go away, that she loved me and would see me again. The next day is when we found out that she was on life support back in Michigan. We flew home immediately. Several days later she was taken off support and passed away.

My parents wouldn't allow me to attend the viewing or the funeral because I was so young. When they returned the day of her burial they were somber and glum.

I said to them "Grandma sure looked pretty in her pink dress. She must have been going to some special party in heaven!" My parents looked shocked, stared at me and then each other. My dad finally said, "Yes, she had a wonderful party to attend and wanted to look beautiful." I just smiled because I already knew. She was wearing the pink dress when she came to visit me. It was much later in life that I learned from them I was indeed correct and that she was wearing a light mauve colored dress in her casket.

At 17, I was as most teen girls; Boy crazy and reckless. My mother gave me her old car to drive around and was in the process of looking for a new one for her. I was just about to leave one day to go over to my boyfriend's house and my mother asked me to drop by her mother's house (Gram) and check on her. She had been calling her all day and there was no answer. My mother and Gram talked about 20 times a day on the phone, so this was very unusual. I agreed and went by the house.

That day changed my life. I found her breathing shallow and unmoving on the floor. She had tried to reach the phone and we suspect she fell - we learned afterwards, she had had a massive stroke. Emergency services were called and my Gram died 25 days later in the hospital as a result from a 2nd stroke.

Never realizing that others didn't see or hear spirits like I did, it never occurred to me that it was odd or scary. Though, I didn't share that information with many. I was raised in a very traditional Lutheran home; Missouri Synagogue, which was more towards the Catholic faith. Hearing voices was frowned upon. Last thing I wanted was to be exorcised.

As a teen, it's pretty hard to talk to your parents about anything and this was going to be even harder. How was I going to explain that I was able to communicate with dead people!? My Gram was not going to leave me alone until I delivered her message to my mom, so I just sat down at the table and said, "Mom, I need to tell you something from Gram." She looked at me as if I had grown two heads but said "Okay."

"Gram says that you really shouldn't put a grave blanket on her grave, she isn't there. She only comes there when you do and hears what you say."

Now my mother was really looking at me oddly but calmly said, "How did she tell you this?"

"In my mind." I mumbled. 'She really likes the Hollyhock flowers you planted in her memory. She knows that you loved it as a girl when she would make you toothpick dolls with the blooms."

The information was something she had never shared with me. I did find out that all of it was completely true. My mother had been debating on putting a blanket on the grave. It was expensive and she asked my Gram if she really wanted one when she would pray at night for a sign. The other message my mother told me was exactly what she had said one night before she fell asleep. Mom told Gram that she was going to plant some Hollyhock flowers in her memory by the porch.

Later in life I started to use my medium-ship as a tool to help others. I found that I could channel these spirits and give details of their deaths, their favorite pipe tobacco, their personality and more. The messages they gave through me helped their families understand that they were not really gone, but still knew about upcoming parties, weddings and such that were occurring long after their deaths.

One of the first parties was for my hair dresser, she was getting married and wanted to have a something fun for entertainment.

I was so nervous about doing well, that about 10 times that night I kept saying.. "Oh man, what if this really is my imagination, I'm going to be SO embarrassed!" I had never done any readings publicly and even though Lauren had already had an impromptu message from her grandfather come through me, I still felt as if I could be wrong. Obviously, even the best mediums still have doubt issues. Why? Because we are spirits, living a human existence! Ego is our "voice of reason". The night went wonderfully and even today, I'm the major attraction for the "Glitz" fundraisers when I come to town. They are constantly doing charity work and helping others through their business. I love you girls!

In May of 2007, while lying down to sleep, I had a vision of my father in a coffin. More like just a flash. I was startled and jumped up in bed. This woke my husband. I was quite upset obviously but I tried to ignore it. I talked to my husband about it, who knew of my abilities. He encouraged me that I should talk to my father.

My father had never really been sick and had just retired after 35 years at Chrysler Motors. Finally he was going to be able to "putter" around the house and enjoy his life. My parents both have a very strong faith in God and yet still believed in my abilities. I chose to tell my father that I had had a "dream" instead of a vision. I suggested that he go to the doctor for a check up. As men do, he just dismissed my warning and talked about doctors being quacks. He joked about it and never gave it another thought.

It was about three months later when my father noticed that every time he would eat, the food would not go down into his stomach and instead came back up. He went to a family physician. After several tests, he was diagnosed with terminal esophageal and stomach cancer, with a large mass blocking the food. (Another confirmation of my ability but a very sad one indeed.) I often thought while he was going through chemotherapy, by his own choice, why did spirit send me this message if I was not to save his life? I know now that it was merely to encourage me to spend more time with him and enjoy his long-winded stories, because he was not long for the earth plane. (Yes my father had PLENTY of those stories!)

My father lived about 8 months following his diagnosis. In that time I hugged him more, I talked about my medium abilities and offered him books to read about the after-life. He really enjoyed "Talking to Heaven" by James Van Praagh and "Forever Ours" by Janis Amatuzio MD.

He, in turn, would tell me about his "visions". That my grandmother, his mother, kept appearing to him but told him it was not yet time to come home. I remember one evening he said that he was walking down a street with a man. This man was shorter and he had to look down to speak to him. My dad also remarked that he felt he knew this man, but could not place him. (It is my father's guide). The man had told him that his mother, Jean was waiting for him just around the next corner and dad said he remembered saying "Well where is she? Can we hurry up?" The man said, "No, it is not yet time for you to see her." This was a great confirmation to me that his guide was telling him; it was not time to go home to the Other Side.

He asked me if I knew when he was going to die. I didn't know the time, but I too, started to see his mother around him. I chose to help my father not to be afraid of his death and console him with what I knew of the Other Side. After a trip to the hospital for dehydration, I came into his room to see him staring out the window, IV pole in hand, and tears down his cheeks. "Dad, what's wrong?"

My dad was one of the strongest men I knew. I'd never seen him cry. Ever. He said to me, "I was just watching the men building the new wing, I miss it. (He was a carpenter all his life) I don't want to die here. It's too cold in here and that man is always moaning." (He motioned to the cancer patient in the next bed).

"I really would just rather jump down the stairwell and get this whole shit over with." I was shocked.
My dad? Thinking about suicide? Never.

"Dad" I said, "What do you want me to do? Anything, I'll help you."

"Get me out of here." he said softly.

I worked in medical at the time as a transcriptionist. I called my staff doctor at the clinic and asked him what to do. He gave me the numbers to several Hospice places. The hospice staff nurse arrived at the hospital in 40 minutes and the paperwork signed. My mom was not happy and said that he needed to stay in the hospital for treatment. She was not ready to let him go yet. "Ma" he said. "I'm dying, we all know that. I don't want to die in here."

I was there to wheel him to the car. Hospice was wonderful. They gave him a bed, walker, pain killers and attention. He thanked me a lot for my help in the few months that I had left with him. By serving his wishes I felt full of love and proud to be of service. (Just a start to what was yet to come in my life as a medium).

He passed away March 14, 2008. It was early morning and I was at home with my family. My mother called at around 7:00 a.m. and I could not tell what she was saying except, "He's gone." Glad that I only lived 5 minutes from my parents; I hurried over to say my goodbyes. I knew he was in the room watching us, but my grief was too strong to "see" him. (Which happens to all of us, even mediums)

Thinking back, it was three days before his death, when he was not really in his body. He would talk about things that didn't make much sense and would stare into nothingness for hours. "How much did the oranges cost?"

"I'm not sure dad why?" I'd answer. He'd reply "What?"

It was Thursday March 13th and my mom needed to run out to the store. She left to watch my dad who was now bed ridden. I sat across from him in a chair just looking at his thin body and hairless head, silently weeping for how sick he had become. He looked up at me and in the most focused voice said "It will be all right. There is no other way it can be." I went over and hugged him, crying harder still. I whispered "I love you." He said. "I love you too kid." as he patted my back. Then his mind drifted off again. That was a message I knew came from his higher soul; comforting me until he could speak no more. He will always be missed on this earth.

I had many life changes after losing my rock, my father. I saw myself writing a book. in a vision and I actually witnessed me signing the book for people as they waited. I saw the colors that you see now on this cover today. I asked my guides *what I was to write about?*

. They said, "You are merely the vessel to transfer our teachings to paper. You do not need to know the content yet. We will channel the information through your hands."

This book is the result of what my guides have requested I write. Whenever possible, I will name the guide or guides, if they so choose. Otherwise, just know that these angelic messages and teachings are to help you all on your spiritual path during your stay here on earth.

Blessings,

Laura Tancy Evans

Greetings and Blessings;

I have been Laura's guide since her dissension to earth. Some people call me a "gate guardian" or "Protector" guide. Most earth body spirits (you) believe that we choose a person to assist on earth. While part of that is correct, it is more the spirit that is to be incarnated that chooses us. More of an earth-like meeting is arranged and our soul groups gather and decide what lessons the incarnate would like to learn on Earth in order to experience greater enlightenment here on this side. (There are levels)

Through each lesson the soul is able to learn a specific lesson such as unconditional love, trust, humility, patience, and truth. These are just a few to be named. Some of us have been on Earth for one or more lifetimes and some have not chosen to incarnate in a body at all.

I chose my name during my earth lessons in body and have decided that name to give to Laura for identification. Names are not important to us here. We all carry the personalities that we had during our "life or lives" on Earth and I, while being fairly stern and reserved, have a humorous side as well. The name I go by is Chief Red Fox Hunting. A name given to me by my Earth father for my cunning in hunting the animal thus named.

In Laura's lifetime, this name is also associated with a comedian and I found it amusing when I gave her this name and she exclaimed that she was being guided by a dead comedian. (Chuckles).

I appear to her in my native dress; buckskin shirt with fox tails adorning it, buckskin leggings, tall moccasin boots and a fur cap. My role is of her guardian. I am the gatekeeper for her.

When she helps people on Earth by speaking to their loved ones on this side, I am the one that brings the soul forward and act as a director so that their message can be delivered to the family that remains in body. I do this if a spirit does not have the energy to be able to communicate. I assist by sharing energy with the spirit. If a specific soul needs to send a message to a person in body, I am there to help the communication flow easily.

Each of you on earth has more than one guide, one that has been with you from your birth and usually one or two more guides that come to you during times when you need assistance. Some may help with your artistic talents such as painting, music, writing and others may help with technological and medical things such as the way of scientists, doctors and more. We are all here to serve you and help. (When requested).

The veil of "unknowing" is starting to lift as more earth souls acknowledge that we exist. That is why there are more "psychics and mediums" showing up. More people are realizing that you all have the ability to hear spirit and with time and the raising of your energies, you all can speak to us here.

I will add more when the time is right. For now, just know that we are always with you. Ask and we will provide assistance.
~Chief Red Fox Hunting aka Red Fox

Red is indeed a character. *grins* He can be very persistent when I need clarification for a client from spirit. As he has said, souls keep their personalities after they return home to the other side. If your father was quiet and did not like to speak to people on earth, chances are, he is not going to want to speak to me because he retains that personality.

Red has such a commanding presence in spirit, he can usually get the information needed to confirm that this is in fact your father speaking to you through me. I call Red my "Spiritual Bouncer".

~ Laura

Finding your spirit guides

A Message from Laura

I have had many clients and friends ask me how to find their own guides and communicate with them. For me, I have always been able to do this but my guides tell me that meditation is the key to raising your vibrational energy and thus making it easier to "hear" your guides. I now teach interactive classes online so that I can help everyone communicate.

Spirit works on a vibrational level that is much more advanced that we do on Earth. A good reference would be how dogs can hear a dog whistle but our human ears cannot. It works the same way for hearing spirit. When you meditate, you focus your mind and still the daily chatter, thus raising your energy vibrations. There are several books on meditations that teach you how to know your guides. Too many times in my young life, I had no references or information to learn to understand my gifts. I never want that to happen to another child or teen or even adult. I have begun creating podcasts for free that will walk you step by step through fear, understanding and actual exercises in order for you too, to work directly with your spirit guides.

There are many tools you can use to help you to connect with the energy of a spirit. During my professional life, I have utilized psychometry*, Tarot cards, pendulums* and billets*. Each of these allows me to connect to the energy of my client in order to contact their deceased loved ones.

Check out my podcast page at

www.mediumlauraevans.podomatic.com

A Message for Those who are Grieving

For those who have experienced the loss of a loved one, let me offer you my love and healing energies. Though it is difficult for you to understand, your loved one is still here. Our spirit-soul is made of energy. Energy cannot be destroyed but only changed. Like particles of water in the air, your loved one is still around you. A mere thought of them and they come. Understand that we may lose our physical body and are unable to communicate as we once did, but by no means have we left you.

My job is to help people on earth to remember what you chose to do when you were born. I cannot however give you a step-by-step detailed map of exactly your purpose because going through all of the pathways is also a way of learning for you. I can point you in the direction but I cannot choose the path for you. Laura knows that one of the lessons she chose to learn is patience. For her to accomplish this, we have helped to set up circumstances which test her. In these tests she can, of course, chose to not wait, not have patience and therefore not learn at that time this important lesson. If she does wait and let divine timing work for the problem, she will know that her patience has afforded her an easier time with much happiness and here (on the other side) we will celebrate her success. Every lesson that is learned gives us great joy! Our mission is to see that each and every one of you completes the lessons you have chosen to experience. When you do, it is a special occasion!

(I will add here that I had a wonderful house I had found on the internet. It was perfect for us. The problem was, we were still in a lease with the apartments and the house was more than we could really afford. I chose to let spirit work for me. I gave it up to them and let it go. Circumstances arose that put us in that house, even 2 months ahead of when we were supposed to move from the apartments and helped us with the financial issue as well. Ah, believing we deserve it is all it takes!)

Most say that life is so hard, why would I choose to experience the loss of a child or a parent in order to learn a lesson? While this may seem cruel to earth bodied spirits, it is a special lesson for both involved. For the child or parent, it could be their soul's way of teaching you unconditional love. Loving without boundaries or limitations, but to love with everything you have no matter what. It could be that you have lost your faith in God/Divine Spirit. By the soul transition, you may again find your center, your divine purpose.

We understand that losing a parent or child is very painful and of course all of us, as your guides, will comfort you and hold you. Your lessons are hard but with the divine light of love, we will help you to feel peace again. We know that life is not easy, but if it were, you could not learn so quickly and return home to your families waiting here! Just like attending a college that is very complex with many hard lessons, you learn more and even more quickly through this.

To reach a higher plane of knowing on this side, these lessons are necessary. You could one day be guiding someone and having experienced what you have on earth now, makes you a more qualified teacher to those souls who need your support and guidance when it is their turn to be born.

Love and Light,   Neidian   (a joy guide)

Is death the end?

Where do we go from here?

In your limited knowledge of the Other Side, due to the unknowing veil, it is hard for us to explain into words where you go. Death, is the beginning of a new journey. You always return to us here, at home. Earth is merely your school, where you learn lessons that you have set out for yourselves. The Other Side is a place of pure love and pure joy.

There is no anger, no judgment, no persecution, no bias and most of all, no ego. We, as your guides, are never disappointed in you. Mistakes, as you call them, are meant to be. These are all part of your learning. There are no mistakes. No accidents. Everything has a purpose. While for some, who are not yet enlightened to this idea, may feel that this is false. That is your choice. You all have the free will.

From my last incarnation on earth, I know that birth is much more painful and traumatic than death. You may suffer pain before death, but actual death, is painless. It is more like floating, free of the confines of your earth body. It can be confusing to some. Most feel the pull to home directly. Others will fight it, to see their family longer. You will always return again to your family on earth. You may visit as often as you like. We never leave you.

Home, as described many times in this book, is full of a pink light. No sun. It is filled with your spirit family as well as friends and animals. A meadow is usually the first thing you will see upon re-entering home. Peaceful, joyful and comforting. It is about 70 degrees and lovely. Some souls, that have had many hard lessons, will go to a type of recovery room. It is similar to your hospitals. We do not give medicines, but we give healing, understanding, joy and love. (and waves of colors)

You will also go through an event of life reflection. This is where you view your last lifetime in full color and in a three dimensional hologram. You will feel all the feelings from earth at this time. You will see how your words or deeds affected others. If you were unkind, you will feel the recipient's pain or sadness from your words or actions. You judge yourself. You judge your own life. No one else. Your guides remain with you during this time. They offer support and love.

Another question raised is about a place called hell. Again, controversy will stem from my next statement; there is no such place. The creation of hell was by humans. I will not go further on this subject, as it is against the free will to do so. There is a level here where spirits who you would believe go to hell, walk. You though, must make your own choices in these matters. When you have come to home, you then will smile and understand.

Humans create their own problems and turmoil. Usually ego based. Focusing on the bad in any event, instead of on what that lesson taught you. An example may be, your car breaks down at 4 a.m. You now must walk, alone in the dark to find help. At the station, you meet a wonderful man. You strike up conversation, and eventually become friends. Later, marry and have children. Was this an accident? Was the car breaking down a horrific event? Do you see? Each thing in your life, leads you forward to more lessons. Life is what you make it; it is all in your perspective.

~ *A collective of energies*

Reincarnation? To be born again. Why?

The answer is simple. To learn more.

When a spirit decides to have another incarnation, there is a large meeting held. All of your spirit family gathers and you and they discuss what you will learn, who you will chose to guide you at different events or stages of your life. It is a well laid plan. You chose who will be your parents, your mates, your siblings, and so on; even, your friends. The lessons are intact. How they are presented can happen in various ways. None of it is a surprise to us, because we remember what we all agreed on. You, do not. This is why you appointed us, to help you from this side. You knew it would not be easy. Through your experiences, your triumphs, your spirit will grow.

Some souls do not wish to return to the earth for various reasons. Many times they would like to work as spirit helpers to those that will again choose an incarnation.

The body, the vessel is carefully chosen as are the handicaps, family circumstances and other challenges. These differences of the body will work to aid you in your lessons that are chosen. To be born without sight and dependant on others to help you, is a lesson of receiving unconditional love, for you to experience having to depend on help and give love to those who have sight. To overcome negative feelings you may have about being born different.

The lessons are more complex but almost impossible to explain to you in earthly words. In all challenges, each spirit around you learns as well as your own spirit.

When you pass someone on the street that has a disability, do not give them your pity. Smile at them for being so strong in spirit. They have taken on a great burden in order to learn and help others learn love and compassion.

~ Red

Guides that are our previous family
~message from Laura

My father promised me just before he died, that he would come and talk to me. I am not sure if he really believed that I could talk to the dead. I gave it a shot and asked that he come to me. On Mother's Day 2009, my father came to me just before I was waking up. I was in the hyponogia state or twilight, just before fully awakening. I saw him in his old jeans and a blue shirt, standing on the beach near his home in Florida. Behind his back he brought out a bunch of lilacs. He kissed my cheek and said in his mind to me "Happy Mother's Day kid!" "The lilacs are for your mom. Tell her I love her, and I love you too!" I sat up with the tingle of his kiss on my cheek. When I asked him later that day. "Hey, what took you so long to come to me!?" He said "What do you mean? I just left!" "Your time it may have been a year, but to us here, there is no time."

I talk to my father all the time since his passing. He was one of those kinds of fathers that always made sure you had gas or money. I would stop by my parent's house on the way to work each morning and he would always say. "Is that gas tank above 1/2?" (He hated it under 1/2 because he said condensation got into the engine and made it run badly). I would always give him the "Yeah dad." He must have been more psychic that I knew. He would say "Here, take this and fill it up."

Many times as I was channeling this book, my father has made sure that I had what I needed when I needed it. Maybe it was God's Will, maybe it was Papa "taking care" of his little girl from beyond.

Faith without seeing

Hello and thank you for picking up this book. We spirit beings have pointed you here for a reason. Know that nothing is by chance. Each path is guided. While the outcome is yours to create, every nudge is spirit giving you that small boost to answer the questions roaming through your mind.

Can you see the wind? If it happens to blows a leaf. What if there is nothing for wind to move, how do you know it exists?
Faith is the same. You on Earth have faith in the Divine or God. You have not seen the Divine Spirit with your earthly eyes, but you still most of you believe that a Higher Power governs over all.

Guides are "heaven-sent". While most of us do not use the term "heaven", we will use it here for purposes to help you to understand that heaven is not a place but more a state of consciousness, another dimension. We guides work through many enlightened masters like Buddha, Christ, the Goddess, etc. What you choose to call the Divine does not matter, but only that you have faith and believe that you are loved and cherished.

We, too, are sent to answer your questions and prayers. Some religions refer to us as "Angels". While everyone does have angelic guidance, not all of us are angels.
Angels have a much higher energy frequency than most and have not lived a life-time on Earth in a body. Except for two, the twins.

They will come when asked for and just as we do, aid you in times of suffering and sorrow. Just as we do, they help in even the smallest of things or at times when you feel the worst.

My message to you is to have faith in us as well as in God, we are all part of the Divine God-head. We are doing the Creator's work. You must only call on your helpers and we will assist you.

Release the fear you may have. Protect your energy with positive light and ask for us, your Divine messengers and we will answer when we can.

Peace and Love

~ A collective of energies

When Opportunity Knocks, Which Door Will You Open?

In your life many lessons need to be completed per your choosing which took place before you accepted to be born onto Earth. In these lessons you will have free will; the power to say yes or no to any given opportunity. We would like you to know that you have the ability to know what will teach you the most and what would be the easier path. Not always is easy the best learning for you.

We guides set up different opportunities and you will be able to pick the path. There may be two waiting jobs for you, one of them does not seem like you will do your best at it, while the other seems the easiest. Most times the hardest and the most uncertain is the way that will teach you self-worth, humility, self-sacrifice and unconditional love.

Even in a love relationship, there are free-will choices for you. We as your guides can give you feelings and impressions about your partner; it is up to you to understand which is best for you in your learning process. There may be Karmic debt owed to a certain soul and therefore this Earth-bodied spirit will be matched with you again in this lifetime in order for one or both of you to figure out the lesson you had previously set out to learn. It could be an issue that was created in a past life that you must now make amends for. If you abandoned your child in another life, possibly your soul chose to be the child of this soul in this life. To pay back the Karmic Debt you created. Even that lesson of sorrow and loss taught you about love, trust and truth. The things that seem bad and terrible are teachings for your soul.

Your guides have many different responsibilities. Some of us are healers, helpers, teachers, joy guides and more. You may call us what you like, just know that we are guiding you always. Ask us for help in choosing your path and we will give you signs to show you which will teach the lessons your soul has asked to learn. I will tell you that when you ask us, be specific. If you want to know if Joe or Tom is best. Best at what? Making you happy? Making more money? Being a father? Give us the question and we will send you the answers.

Not only can we help in major events but just for small luxuries in your life. If it is cold and you would like a parking spot closer to the door of the grocery store, just ask. If you decided to go in to buy one thing and now have several but did not get a buggy, ask us and we will direct you to a buggy. We want your experiences on Earth to be happy and joyful. Where one door closes, another will open.

Believe.

~ Chief Red Fox Hunting

I can't even count the number of times the above has happened to me. I swear, I go in for sugar and end up with about seven other things. Now my arms are full and I'm kicking myself for not grabbing a cart or buggy. I say, "Hey, can you guys get me a buggy?", I will walk to an aisle, maybe two down from the one I am in, and there it is. Empty and alone. Seemingly placed there by invisible hands, just for me!

Your path?

Those whose hands sit idle, waiting to learn their paths. You need not wait. Trusting your center (solar plexus) is all you need. Do not think you are forsaken in your quest for the path. It is right before you. Open your mind. Listen to us. You may have forgotten your celestial charts, but this is why we were in contract with you; to be there in your unknowing, to be there in your strife. We are here. We are helping you. Trust in our guidance young ones. Serving you is our pleasure.

Who are we? so many ask. We are your friends from past lives, your family in this and the days of old. We are your soul group; your ethereal family, guiding you always. As set out before your birth we made that contract with you and you with us. There is nothing by chance. While the lessons remain, the way the lessons are taught are changing, ever constant, but the lesson does not change. It is you that have chosen these lessons to learn. To ascend higher on this plane when your time on earth is through. You can sometimes hear us speaking to you. Though you feel it is only a buzzing in your ears. Our vibrations are so much higher. Raise yours, lift up your spirit and you will hear us.

(Meditation raises your vibrations to hear spirit.)

~ *The boys (my group of guides)*

When you feel you have failed, realize that you have not in our eyes. We understand that the lessons on earth are hard and can be very monumental to you because you are not able to see the whole spectrum. When you have a day that seems to go entirely wrong, know that this was a lesson for you. Possibly for strength, or to see the good in your life, amidst the pain.

We will never abandon you, we hold you tight. We are there in joy and in sorrow. Without the bumps in the road, you would never appreciate it when that road becomes smooth.

Angelic Hands

Laura's path for this lifetime is to teach and help others learn that the light dwells within them. She is our voice when you are too busy to listen or cannot seem to sort out the chatter at this time. If you ask us for guidance but just cannot seem to "hear" our answers, we will send you to a soul like Laura. She will give you the answers we have been trying to. Psychics and Mediums are God's earth-angels. Not all walk the path of truth and honesty and sadly the name "psychic" has become synonymous with fraud and charlatan. If you get a feeling about someone and it is a feeling of mistrust when you sit down for a reading; stand back up and walk out. We are always trying to steer you clear of misfortune. Listen to that inner voice. It is us, calling out to you.

You are psychic, every one of you on earth. You are all capable of speaking and hearing us here on this side. It's just a matter of finding your quiet place and letting yourself hear. You are not mad, insane or making it up, you are not losing your mind. We are here. We are everywhere at once.

Feel the tickle on your cheek. Is it the wind? or maybe angel's wings. See a sunset and know deep inside that the joy you feel is our love, filling you up, hugging you from beyond.

Do not only turn to us only in times of strife, know us in your everyday. Feel us pour out our love for you, our pride in you and our awe of you. You have chosen to be born. That in itself is a wonderful, beautiful thing. It takes a very strong soul to be born to earth. You have the power to overcome so much. We, a legion of angels, are behind you. Ask and it is given. It may not be exactly what you pictured, but know that we remember what you do not. That is why we were chosen by you, because you felt that we would be the best guides and mentors for your life lessons.

Listen to your heart beating, feel the energy of your soul within you now. You are all being called to help one another find the light inside. Focus on your spirit now, listen to it. You want to know your purpose here on the earth. Listen. The hours grow short, now is the time to take action, to connect to the universal energies and know thy path. I am with you, we are with you. To know thyself is to know God. The Divine. Ask and it is given. Not always in your wish of timing, but in divine timing. Keep silent and listen. Your soul is speaking. Quiet your mind. Breathe deeply. Align your energy with ours. Blessed Be.

~

Note:

As my guides and angels have said, they are available to us at any time. You just need to ask. For our personal guides and Archangels, they deal with our mundane. Our car, computer, and the issues we may be having in a relationship or job questions.

For more spiritual questions, I call to my Ascended masters and Universal masters. Merlin, Isis, Ganesh and the more famous Ascended Masters and spiritual teachers of our time, like Buddha and Jesus.

For me, there are still unanswered questions, even though I have the ability to contact spirit and see the Other Side; some things are meant to be unknown to us as spirits in a human body. I feel that if we knew how great it all was, we'd find ways to go home, like step in front of a bus or something drastic. The veil of unknowing is there to protect us, to keep us on our tasks.

If you find yourself wondering why you chose to come here, try learning numerology. It is a wonderful guide to know why you were born. I'm a life path of 9. I'm here to teach and to be a humanitarian. I have the "save the world" syndrome! Ha ha! There are many great books on the subject available. This helps a lot to know where you need to be heading to complete your major theme here on earth. Astrology is another great example of learning your path, your lessons and possibly who you came here to help.

Healing the World with Joy

To follow your path at this time will bring you closer to God/the Divine. Powerful forces are working now toward a Universal shift. Come March of 2012, there will be signs of our work upon the Earth. Helping other light workers to enlighten the masses. Joy and love are the emotions that will bring those beings who feel lost and abandoned out of the murky depths of self-destruction. I am asking those who are reading this book to rub your hands together now, create the energy between them, and send this loving energy to the earth.; to the people on it. Share with them the positive flow of love and joy. While you each alone are one person, together, you are an army of light. We cannot heal the masses without you. We can only inspire you to help your fellow beings out of the madness that they themselves have created.

~ Angels of the Divine Purpose

Call to us

If you feel disparaged, remember always to call on us. Angels of Light surround you and lift you from your darkness. You are never alone in the world. We find it very saddening when beings cry out, "I am so alone!" If only you would quiet your minds, open your heart and feel the energy surrounding you, you would know that not one being born to earth is ever alone. In your worst times of sorrow, despair and depression, we envelope you in our loving auras of light and kiss your soul with such compassion. Your loved ones on this side are with you as well. Our hope is that you learn to feel us in your every day. To simply acknowledge that we are here will lift an immense burden upon you. Seek us. Know us. You will walk proudly, with us at your side.

Lessons from Raven Blackwater
My guide

Laura: I asked Raven in meditation, "Who are you? Who were you to me before?" This is what she said…

I am part of your soul family. We once ruled a kingdom together as what you will call mystics. Our position in the kingdom was of honor and high esteem. I am your guide now, chosen by you before you came back to another lifetime to learn more. You chose to serve humanity this time, to be more neutral in your guidance to release that Karma created from the one we shared. Power, like a drug consumed you. You took the position you held and used it for ill work, ordering the deaths of many were one of your deeds. In this incarnation, you are balancing that with helping others to learn their lessons here, being the gap between the dimensions and spreading positive vibrations instead of harmful ones. I am here to work with you, again, but from this side. I have many things to learn as well but chose not to be so brave to take another body. In time, I will ask you to be my guide in a body life. As it is to be, so we shall continue to serve. Blessed Be Sister.

Laura: I also understand recently that I am going through a lesson of judgment; by not judging others and to not allow the words and actions of others to mold me; now knowing that the only judge in my life is me and my Creator. No one else has the power to tell me who and what I am, nor do I have the power to tell others who and what they should be, as a connection between the worlds.

I strive to give messages from loved ones, to help others understand that energy does not die, but in the same token, I am not here to tell them they must forgive a killer, or love an enemy. Those are their lessons. I can only suggest that they move forward by doing so, but I cannot judge them if they do not.

Free will, freedom of choice, will remain; in life and so in death.

∽

Love is like a candle in the darkness. It spreads out and illuminates. Love is the answer to many questions we ask. Love is the universal thought, the one emotional energy that can transcend time and space. Love is the reason we are born and love is the reason we continue on after death of the body. We all search to know love, in a mate, in a pet, in a family. Love comes from inside you and emanates out. With love, all things are possible. Many quotes in your lifetime were guide inspired. Many teachings you have about love and the lesson of it came from this side. Love on your dimension is difficult to remain constant because of the darkness, the negative, the pain and the sorrow. We do not have those feelings and emotions here. Therefore we choose to be born to body, to reconnect with them; to find love in everything, no matter how dark the day. I can liken it to being lost in a jungle of despair, and love is the compass that points true North. If you can find a glimmer of hope/love in your darkness, then you plant a seed. Allow that seed of love to grow within you; reaching up towards the sky. It is your salvation, your light. Remember to love, to find love in your darkest hour, and you will find the God-head within.

~Raven Blackwater

Laura: Why did you all choose to write this book through me? There are so many being written at this time on the same subjects and by guides like you. How is this book different?

You are the reason. As another part of your teachings and lessons on your incarnation, this book will resonate to others like you, on similar journeys. No one is on the same lessons, but your book will reach those that need to hear these words. There are others who are being guided to write as well, they will also teach a group of souls with their words. The answer is simple, we chose you to teach the ones who are drawn to your book. The other writers and mediums, will teach other souls who are drawn to their books. Many will read both. It is as it should be. Know that you have a divine purpose to teach. That is your lesson.

~Raven Blackwater

Laura: She sometimes makes no sense to me! I think I understand what she means by the above paragraph. That even though there are many books like mine, the energy of this book will attract certain souls that are looking for these answers. Maybe the way they are speaking to you in this book is different from others who channel guides. I am not sure; I am still here, in body, learning just as all of you are! I read these paragraphs and learn as well.

I asked Raven today to give me some information about what she looked like on earth when we lived in that lifetime, what she enjoyed doing in her time away from the job we both shared. Below is her answer to me:

In that lifetime, I had black hair, long to my midsection. My eyes were brown/gold, almond shaped and my face was small. The body I wore was thin and toned, my legs seems too long for me though. (She laughs) Special garments were fashioned for me because of, which I viewed as an imperfection. I wore a band type marking on my right arm and another on my left. This was a symbol of my leadership and also of my talents in the arts. You and I enjoyed many activities together. We would paint and fashion garments. Not all of our time was spent on control. Do you remember Egypt my sister? Does it call to you still? (She smiles knowingly)

~ Raven Blackwater

Those that question our existence or our purity of nature, you must only ask us to answer a simple question "Are you of God?"

The true guides and guardians will answer immediately in the affirmative. A wayward spirit, a trickster, a rogue cannot answer yes to this question. They have not yet been in the presence of this Divine energy and governed by our laws are unable to lie when this question is asked. While yes, the original soul has been part of the God-Head for many eons, the spirit of the last incarnation may have not yet accepted the lessons learned while in body. The cruel actions and deeds of some spirits must first be forgiven by that soul. If they cannot do this, they do not ascend and arise into the presence of our God-Light. Do you understand?

Have no fear of these beings, it gives them power over you. Harm can only come to you if you allow them to control you in body and mind. Treat them as a bothersome insect in your ear and fan them away. Be stern. Demand that they leave your energy and go back from whence they came. Say a prayer of protection for yourself and think of it no more.

You have us here for help and aid, but we cannot do everything that is requested. Realize it is not for our lack of want but more that in order for you to learn, there are some things that must be learned through difficulty.

You have the body, you have the power. Remember this always. No person, spirit, animal or being can control you if you do not allow yourself to relinquish this control to them. Negative emotions can feed the darklings. Be strong my earth spirits, be strong!
~ Raven Blackwater

Questions and Answers with Spirit

I have decided to ask my friends who are part of a spiritual posting board to help me pose some questions to the spirit realm and have the spirits answer them. I hope that these are some questions you have been wondering about as well.

These are a collection over many years. This book is based on my journal that began in 1997.

Q: My friend is in a difficult relationship. Her boyfriend has been cheating on her. Now he has decided to come back and wants to try again with her. What is your advice?

A: **While each relationship is different, she can be very controlling and treats him as a child and not a partner. She needs to understand that a love relationship is about sharing and working together. Once the control is relinquished, she will begin to see that in order to create the loving environment she has wanted, she must accept his faults and know that he is also on this earth to learn. He did not want a love relationship with the other woman; he only wanted her to see that he needed something more from her. This was a wake up call to her ego. While this was a painful lesson, there is hope for them.**

~ *Chief Red Fox Hunting*

Q: Some of us wonder why there are psychics in the world who seem above us all. More in tune, more aware. Are they chosen to be better at receiving than others for a reason?

A: It may seem that the psychics and mediums you refer to have an advantage that most humans do not, this is not the case. These beings have a much evolved soul or higher self. If you were to look at their lives before the fame, you will see that they started out very much like most children. The fact that their parents or someone of authority were understanding and encouraging helped them to ascend much faster. Possibly even these children were abused and neglected. They turned inward for comfort. They found us early on. This ability is available to all. While you have it here at home, you have forgotten your lessons before birth. You too can be as intuitive as they are. Open up your heart, allow us to communicate to you. Do not fear your information. We are here to guide you in whatever you wish to accomplish. They may be figureheads but there are hundreds of thousands of beings just like them walking this earth. You too can become a light worker.

~ Immanuel

Q: What is so important about meditation? Do we really need to meditate in order to hear our guides?

A: As you walk the earth, you take in many thoughts. These can be things like, "Did I remember to pay the gas bill? Where did I put my favorite sweater?" Maybe your negative friend calls and tells you all about her terrible day. Now you have all of these things running in your active mind. How can you hear us through all of that chatter? You can't. Meditation is key to quieting the chatter in order to open up your mind-hearing. When you relax and clear, you raise your vibrations of energy, that more closely match our higher energies here. We in turn, lower our vibrations to equal that of yours. Now, we have an open channel. Like a radio station on earth. The more closely you are to the signal, the more you will receive. Our vibrations are also so much higher because we do not have the density of the earth body. *By us lowering our vibrations and you (through meditation) raising yours, we can communicate.*

Q: Why is it so hard for some to open up with their abilities and for others, it's a piece of cake? ~ Grapevine_100 Peoria,IL

A: For most that are struggling with abilities it is about the fear of what they will find. The fear that finally knowing what is wrong in their lives means that they will have to make drastic changes in order to "fix" themselves. My suggestion is to relax more and trust your inner voice. We are trying very hard to connect to you. We will never stop trying. Do not have fear, it keeps you from the help you so much desire.

Q: Why are you and the other guides following us mortals around, guiding us, watching out for us, advising us, when someone of your equal status, our own spirit, is within in us? ~ Dann from Washington State

A: Upon your ascension to the earth plane, there was a meeting between several of us. You included. We are all old friends but you do not remember this. It is imperative for your growth that you do not recall what we discussed before your "birth" into body. Since you cannot remember what you chose to learn, you have assigned us, your spirit guides to help you without interfering in your lessons. Some of us had bodies on earth at some time. Your angels or higher spirit guides have not had a body and are more ascended. They keep you from imminent danger when it is not yet your time to come home. They are available to you at any time in your life.

~ Chief Red Fox

Q: Is it possible that there are certain people who no matter how much they meditate are not meant as part of their path to actually have one on one sessions with their guides or main guide for guidance? Instead have constant lucid dream or visual experiences that are to figure out the meaning of instead? ~ Sophia

A: The first part of your question is no. You are capable. Your ego is on overdrive and though you feel you are raising your energy enough, your ego is keeping you afraid of us. Do not worry, we are working hard to lower our vibrations to meet yours. It will happen. Keep talking to us.
The second question is we do come to you in dreams when we cannot penetrate the veil of your ego self. It is the way we can bypass your body's defense system. Keep trying. It will happen! We will never give up on you!

~ Archangel Raguel

Q: Why is it so difficult for people to accept and understand that indeed there are normal people with special gifts and that we don't always have to look for help in any particular formal religion when there is someone right besides you who can help you find your answers without condemning? ~ Star_Light

A: You are all on different levels. Just like here at home, you each grow and learn differently. Those who are condemning of your abilities are on a much lower frequency and have not allowed themselves to see the light within. Those even who claim to all that they know "God" and are following in His ways, are actually going through the motions like sheep following a shepherd. They have not found the divine within. People who do not judge others for their beliefs, who do not try and change you because you do not match what they think is right, are the most enlightened souls. Your question about the religion is hard for me to put into words. Let me say this. There is no one "TRUE" religion. We are all part of the God-head and all one.

~ Immanuel

Q: How do we know if we are on the right path in our lives?

It is a tug, in your solar plexus area that tells you "something" is not quite right. We give you these hints to help you navigate. Depression is another sign that you are off path. If you feel lost and depressed, it may just be that you have wandered off the path. No matter how many forks you take, you will always come back to your path. We know the lessons you have chosen to learn. The people (souls) you have recruited to help you along the way. Doing good for others, saying a kind word or just smiling is redirecting you to the right path. Ask us. We will give you signs.

Q: Why do beings become addicted to alcohol and drugs? What are they hiding from?

A: These souls are usually new to the earth's plane and similar to children on your planet, they haven't yet learned the way to properly deal with pain and fear. Some souls choose parents who have the same issues that they as adult beings are faced with now. The soul wished to overcome these obstacles and find the light inside. Many young souls do not realize that while this challenge is a wonderful learning experience, which they may not yet be advanced in soul enough to break the bonds of this addiction. We as their soul mentors do try and help them before they are born to choose a smaller lesson at first to become accustomed to being an earth-spirit, but they feel they are ready and choose to take on this task. We are merely advisors; free will still governs here as well.
So as to answer your question, they are hiding from themselves; their own perception of failure. While they may lack skills, we are all still here on the Other Side, providing them support. They need to call to us for that support. We cannot step in and intervene without being asked. As mentors and teachers, we only want to see them succeed. Call to us when you have lost your way. We are here, listening and waiting.

~ Beings of the Divine Purpose

Q: How do we remember the lessons we chose before our birth? Can we?

A: The tools to find this answer are given to you. Speaking to us with your mind. Noticing signs that we are giving you in your daily life. You must open up and realize that while your life is not predestined, there are no accidents. A feather, a coin, a butterfly, a bird. All of these are symbols to you at times in your life when you are seeking guidance. Be aware. Be alert. Search for the answers within. Most earth-beings are born to spread love, kindness, peace, truth and trust.

Your natal chart is another way you can see what lessons you have chosen to work on in this life. We do give you maps. It is up to you to use them.

There are many other lessons to be chosen as well. If you chose charity, to help others less fortunate, we will present circumstances for you to choose to be charitable. The dirty man on the corner of a busy street, homeless and hungry. Will you give him food? Will you help him find shelter? Trust in our guidance to show you your lessons. Yes, there are many who set out to falsely resemble these lost souls. This is why each of you has "intuition". Look at the man. Do you feel sorrow? Do you feel remorse? or do you feel something is not right? You know deep inside which is the right answer. Trust in your heart. There are children greatly in need of a positive role model. Will you spend some time with them? Will you tutor them? Teach them a game? This is a lesson is charity. Giving of yourself, without need for compensation or reward.

If your lesson is patience, you may have conversed here on this side with your "children" who decided to help you with this lesson. They may be born to you with strong wills, spiteful mouths and troublesome behavior. You may look at this as a curse. Instead, they are tools for your lesson. If you find that you are losing patience with them. Step back from the situation and look within. You will find the lesson and the tools to help you to work through it.

~ Beings of the Divine Purpose

Q: Why are people on earth suffering from poverty, sickness and hunger? Is this punishment?

A: Higher souls may choose to be born onto the earth just for the purpose of providing lessons for those who wish to accomplish charity and compassion. The souls that are born into this suffering know before hand that they will incur much hardship. They go into the body with full understanding of this. Because of the veil of forgetting though, these souls do not recall why they chose to suffer in this way. Every one of you can do just a little to help them. It helps your soul grow and ascend to higher vibrations. Treat it as a lesson for all of mankind to help the entire world with charity and compassion. It may not be clear to you now, but when you come home, you will fully understand this.

Q: My aunt died a few days ago. Is it possible to go to a medium to get messages from her?

There is a transition period after crossing over. This may be hours, days, weeks or many years to you on earth. This Other Side has no concept of time. While yes it may be possible, it does not always happen. After coming from such a negative place with hard lessons and pain, your spirit needs a time to adjust to the loving energies of home. There is a place much like a hospital here. You are given love, positive energy, cleansings and color work. Many guides, angels and caregivers attend to you. Some of them were medical professionals in their lives at one time. We do the things we enjoy most at home too. There is also a life review that takes place. Your aunt's spirit may be too weak or low in energy to be able to contact the earth plane at this time. Have patience and she will send you messages of her safe arrival at home.
~ Red Fox Hunting

Another guide/spirit moves in and adds to this:

It is hard to explain to you on the earth plane that there are 7 levels. Each level has many dimensions in it. Level 1 is where you enter first. This looks more to you like your earth home and helps greatly in your transition. Anything you wish is possible here. Second levels can communicate and work with mediums on your plane and 1st levels are where the spirits who are not very evolved go or those just passed. It is where we help you to understand where you are. Make you comfortable and work with you. Everyone spends some time at level 1. Those who are what you call bad or evil, spend a vast amount of time on level 1. This is the level that you on earth, who do not understand proper communication with this side, pull in spirits that long to be back on earth. They manipulate earth beings, scare them and even control them. This is the plane that spirits with no remorse over taking human life reside.

If the soul of your aunt was more highly evolved, it is not that she does not wish to contact you, but has moved on to higher levels - where communication to earth is not possible. She may send you signs, songs, or other messages.

Level 2 is similar to Level 1, in that you can create anything you want. Home, worldly possessions, a home on the beach; it is all available to you with a mere thought.

The 3rd level is for spirits/souls that have made a profound contribution on earth. They have inspired and guided in love and light. Some souls, like these, progress from the healing stage to level 3 without ever needing to be on level 2. We all arrive on level 1 for a period of time though; it is like our sorting bay.

Q: What do spirits do at home? Are there jobs? Where do you live?

There are jobs and we do work, but we can be many places at once. We can guide you and still perform other duties simultaneously. Jobs just like on earth exist here; Gardening, carpentry, doctors, lawyers, surgeons. Although many of these things are not built as your items are. We use our minds. If we wish to craft, the materials are just a simple thought away. We enjoy many of the things you do on earth, but in a different sense. Obviously, no surgery is required, but you may still have the means to perform these tasks. It is hard for you to understand this and there are really no words to explain.

We live in our dream home. If you love a cabin in the woods; you will have it, a beach front home. You now live in it. It is everything you have ever needed or wanted on the earth plane.

Q: What can this book tell people about our lives here on earth and what we can do to make our lessons easier?

A: Your lives are all conjoined. Each separate but yet part of a whole. Spreading love and kindness throughout, ripples into the next person's energy and thus creates a shock-wave of goodness and happiness. Thus it is the same for negative energy. If you dwell on having a bad day, the universe will manifest more of what you think you deserve. Thoughts are actions not yet set into motion. Change your thoughts; change your day, your week, and your life.
Your lessons do not need to bring you pain. They are chosen by you to help your spirit evolve and learn feelings and emotions that cannot be taught here on this side. Struggles, which some may choose not to see, are actually brought on by your own negative thinking. Learning to find another way to release issues that are blocking the lesson at hand, will result in an enlightening experience for your soul.

~Spirits of the Third Ray

Q: What are chakras?

A: *The meridian of the spirit and body. When these energy discs are clogged, it leads to imbalance with the spirit and the body. We have instructed many light workers on the ways to clear and energize these discs. Reiki is also another way to balance these meridians and evoke healing and love between the flesh and the soul. Anyone of you has the ability to balance your meridians, do this to align your spirit to your body.*

~Spirits of the Third Ray

Q: Do our pets join us in heaven?

Pets do join you on the Other Side. Even those from different life times. All animals go to the "Summerland's" or "Heaven" and live in perfect harmony. A lion with a lamb, a fox with a mouse. There is no need for food and therefore they do not have the same drive as they did on earth. Know that your beloved pets that have gone before you are patiently waiting until you come Home again!

~ Chief Red Fox Hunting

Q: What about people with Down's syndrome or disfiguring disabilities? Are they being punished?

They are among the few highly evolved souls that chose to "expedite" their soul growth by coming to earth with a disability. There is no punishment from the Other Side. You choose every thing you experience on earth. The lessons are set, but the ways to the lessons are free will. They are here to help us overcome prejudice, hatred and so much more. Smile when you see these souls, they know more than you think they do!

Q: What is a soul mate? Is this a lover? Or can it be another person like sister, friend?

A: Souls that have aligned together in a contract. You have many soul mates and yes, it can be a lover, a friend, a father, or more. There is a special ignition center that you and this mate will share. It will be an immediate "knowing". That soul mate is to help you in a lesson. This can be from humility to patience. The term "soul" mate, just means that you have agreed before birth to help each other on earth; in one form or another. Your sister, your son, your father, your neighbor, yes, each can be a soul mate.

~ Angels of the Third Ray

Q: How do guides communicate?

There are many ways and music is one way that we connect to you. The words of the song or even in the instruments themselves. Pay attention to the signs we are giving you. Road signs, animal messengers, numbers, feathers, pennies and just an energetic touch. All of these are the way we communicate to you. Remember that we are never far from your side. Main guides and joy guides are with you life long. Look into the night sky. See the picture painted there. A gift of home to you. Learn your lessons well. Grow in the knowledge set forth for you on earth. Joy is a great teacher. You do not have to experience pain to grow. Remember this.

You have not lost your loved ones. They do not die. Just the body dies, the vehicle or house of the soul. You, your soul and your spirit are eternal. You will again return home with us. Breathe deeply children. Your life is but a short time to us. So many things to learn and work through. In your heart is the seed of remembrance. Your home key. If you still your mind and listen inwards. You can remember home. Remember us.

As a guide. It is our service to help others grow in the light. To learn about guides, angels, spirits and more. We connect those on earth to those here on this side. Grief can interrupt the messages you are receiving from us. In time, you will hear.

Our goal, our mission, Laura and I - is to help those in need. Those seeking answers. She is the medium, the conduit or as she says "The spiritual cell phone" to the other side. Through me and her other guides, we work hand in hand to bring clear communication to her for you.

Maintaining a low vibration for us is difficult. We knew upon taking the role of guide, that this would not be easy. This is why most guides have had many incarnations on earth, to learn about being in body. It takes a highly evolved spirit to bridge the gap between the worlds. You all have guides, every one of you. They too, can connect you to this side. We are able. It is our duty to serve.

~ Chief Red Fox Hunting

*Lost and alone you feel you are searching in an unending sea of sorrow
Do not cry my precious ones, you are not alone.
We stand at your side, we hold you in your tears,
Dance in your joy and celebrate your accomplishments.*

*Floating with you in the ethereal, we are your friends, your lovers, your family, your teachers.
Giving you constant loving thoughts, sending you healing energies and picking you up when you fall.*

Ask and it is given. In the Divine's timing.

*Align your soul bodies' everyday with that of your humanness.
Do your meditations to be more in tune with us here.*

Peace to all and blessed be.

~ Unknown

Note from the author:

So many people ask me about the Other Side. It is a wonderful place that does not know sorrow or pain. There are colors so vibrant that we cannot even begin to imagine what they look like. There is no sun, but instead a pink hue over everything! My spirit guides call this the God light or God spark. There is no night and we don't need sleep there! Sleep is for our body and brain - which we no longer have at Home. We sill have cookouts, dances, parties and other celebrations just like we do here on earth. We even have food and drinks there! The food is only for socialization because we no longer need food to run our bodies. There are animals that have been long extinct on earth, living and communing together. My guides tell me that it is a place unlike anything we could ever picture. There is a sense of oneness that is not known here. We come here to learn because of the negativity of this planet. Yes, there will always be turmoil here, because it was created as a school to overcome these obstacles and learn to love unconditionally, help others through our "inner God light" and become one with everything. We set out lessons before we are born into flesh. While the lessons may vary, it is all based on love. Without the negative, we would never learn to be positive even in the midst of darkness. There is a Hall of Records where the Akashic Records are held, from everyone's past lives and this one. In spirit, we can reflect on them at any time.

Remember to take time to love your family and friends. Do something good for you and someone else everyday. Start healing by forgiving yourself for being human, with human emotions and human feelings. Forgive others for their wrongful deeds for they too, are learning lessons. Remember to smile at a total stranger. This lights up your "soul" and helps you to remember that our Home is a place of pure love and pure joy. Help others remember this too by your positive actions.

During the writing of this book, I have learned much about our suffering here on earth. While all the time I thought that pain and sorrow were just part of learning, I now understand that with the right mind set, we can choose to look at things another way. We are here for such a short time compared to our eternity on the other side. Our loved ones know that we soon will join them in this perfect home and all be reunited again.

Death is one of those transitions that always seems to make people think that this is a punishment. In fact, it is a great celebration; a time to go home to our spirit families. I still do not know all the answers and spirit assures me that it is not my time to know such things, but I hope that in publishing this, it will help people to think differently about tragedy and start looking for that proverbial silver lining in all that we do. Doing one good deed a day is now what I aim to do. Rippling out positive!

Thanks to all the angels, spirits and guides who have helped my hands to write this. I hope that you have enjoyed their lessons as much as I have.

Many Blessings,

Medium Laura Evans

LVX